KT-545-930

Bristol Libraries

1800028967

BRITAIN SINCE 1948

Popular Culture

Stewart Ross

WAYLAND

BRISTOL CITY LIBRARIES	
AN1800028967	
PE	01-Sep-2008
C941	£12.99

First published in 2008 by Wayland

Copyright © Wayland 2008

Wayland
338 Euston Road
London NW1 3BH

Wayland Australia
Level 17/207 Kent Street
Sydney, NSW 2000

All rights reserved

Editor: Katie Powell
Designer: Phipps Design

British Library Cataloguing in Publication Data

Ross, Stewart
Popular culture. - (Britain since 1948)
1. Popular culture - Great Britain - History - 20th century - Juvenile literature
2. Social change - Great Britain - History - 20th century - Juvenile literature
3. Great Britain - Social conditions - 20th century - Juvenile literature
I. Title
306'.0941'09045

ISBN 978 0 7502 5373 4

Printed in China

Wayland is a division of Hachette Children's Books,
an Hachette Livre UK company
www.hachettelivre.co.uk

Picture acknowledgements: Advertising Archives: 19. Bettmann/Corbis: 22.
Jonathan Butler/Photosport/Topfoto: front cover & 23. Torrey Byerholt/Rex
Features; 15. Classicstock/Topfoto: 21. Fortean/Topfoto: 18. John
Garrett/Corbis: 20. Rune Hellestad/Corbis: 29. Hodder Children's Books: 26.
Hulton-Deutsch/Corbis: 5, 10, 11. Peter Kingsford/Topfoto: 24.
Gideon Mendel/Corbis: 16. Barbara Michaels/Topfoto: front cover & 14.
Ian Monro/Topfoto: 6. Pictorial Press/Alamy. © 2001 Warner Brothers: 27.
Picturepoint/Topham: 9. Popperfoto/Getty Images: 7. 13. Topfoto: 4, 8, 12.
Wayland: 17, 28. Janine Wiedel/Alamy: 25.

Every effort has been made to clear copyright. Should there be any
inadvertent omission please apply to the publisher for rectification.

The website addresses (URLs) included in this book were valid at the
time of going to press. However, because of the nature of the Internet,
it is possible that some addresses may have changed, or sites may have
changed or closed down since publication. While the author and Publisher
regret any inconvenience this may cause the readers, no responsibility for
any such changes can be accepted by either the author or the Publisher.

Contents

Words in **bold** can be found in the glossary.

Britain in 1948

In 1948, Britain was still recovering from the Second World War, which had ended three years before. The country was short of food. New clothes and furniture were scarce and bombed homes had not yet been replaced. In many hearts the unhappiness of wartime death, injury and separation lingered on. Yet the British were no more miserable than today – there were many ways of having fun!

The Pictures and the Pub

Television was still extremely rare, and going to the cinema – known as the 'flicks' or the 'pictures' – was ten times more popular than nowadays. *Gentlemen's Agreement* was the voted best film of 1948 but more people probably enjoyed the rip-roaring western *Red River*, starring John Wayne. Sport was in full swing again and hundreds of thousands flocked to football matches and horse race meetings. There were always circuses and fairs, too, and visits to the theatre, opera and ballet for those who could afford it. For most adults, though, the normal evening out was a trip to the local pub.

Voices from history

'Another early post war relaxation was the recognition… that girls existed. Exchange dances were arranged with… girls' schools, for the sixth formers. Apart from youth clubs, opportunities to meet girls were rather few and so these "blind date" events were eagerly anticipated…These were enjoyable occasions, although they tended to be rather formal and not very relaxed. Certainly our Head… never looked at ease.'

John Holmes remembers his time at an all-boys school in North London, from the Old Haberdashers' Association website.

Down the pub, 1950s style • *Notice the smoke, the hairdos and the men's caps. In some ways the picture is unusual, though. Groups of women did not often go into pubs on their own.*

4

▲ **Big band, big dance** • *Couples dancing to Ted Heath's Band at the Hammersmith Palais in the 1950s. The dance style is very formal compared with today.*

Workers' Playtime

Eating out, except perhaps buying fish and chips wrapped in newspaper, was expensive. The family meal, especially at the end of the day and Sunday lunchtime, was a regular ritual in most homes. This helped family members stay in touch with each other. The meal might be followed by reading, playing cards or a board game like *Monopoly*. Better-off homes had wind-up gramophones that played fast-spinning records with a steel needle. And there was always the radio to listen to. The BBC, the only official broadcaster, offered a small range of programmes.

CHANGING TIMES

In the late 1940s, radios picked up three BBC stations (the Home Service, the Light Programme and Third programme), and Radio Luxembourg. See how many programmes you can find on a radio at home today. It is probably nearer 50.

Workers' Playtime, which came from a factory, had been started during the war to help keep people cheerful. Planned to last for just a few weeks, it ran for 23 years and was finally axed in 1964.

Popular Culture in the Home

Over the last 60 years our homes have changed a great deal. Take the radio, for example. Called a 'wireless', it used to be a large and quite expensive wooden box that had to be plugged in and took ages to warm up. Now it is small, cheap and portable. On the other hand, many things we do at home have hardly changed at all. We still wash, sleep and eat there, and from time to time we still have fun events like parties.

SOUNDBITES
Around 18 million viewers regularly watched the 26 episodes of the 1960s BBC TV drama *The Forsythe Saga*. When it was shown on Sunday evenings, pub owners and priests complained that no one was coming to their pubs and churches.

More Choice
The biggest change in what goes on at home is in the range of choices open to us. By the end of the 1950s, for instance, it was quite normal for homes to have a TV, although there were only two channels to watch: BBC or ITV. Within ten years there were three channels. Then came Channel 4 and, in the 1990s, multi-channel satellite TV.

TIMELINE

1948	The board game *Scrabble* is **patented**
1954	The first transistor (portable) radio goes on sale
1960	Lego goes on sale for the first time
1976	*The Muppets* TV programme appears
1981	750 million people worldwide tune in for the wedding of Prince Charles and Lady Diana Spencer
1997	**Tamagotchi** pets first go on sale
2007	High Definition Television is launched

▲

The battle on screen • *Some people complain that modern computer games cut children off from friends and family. Do you agree?*

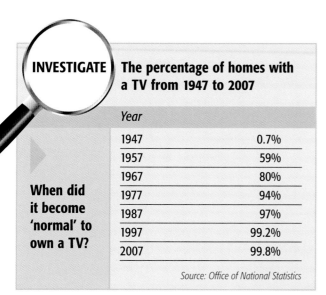

INVESTIGATE

When did it become 'normal' to own a TV?

The percentage of homes with a TV from 1947 to 2007	
Year	
1947	0.7%
1957	59%
1967	80%
1977	94%
1987	97%
1997	99.2%
2007	99.8%

Source: Office of National Statistics

We may eat more and better food, but a traditional Christmas dinner is basically the same now as it was in 1988 and back in 1958. Birthday parties still have cakes and candles. Card games, like **patience**, **whist** and **bridge**, have not changed, nor have many popular board games such as *Cluedo*, which was invented in 1946.

Popular games • Card games have never lost their popularity. The man on the left of this 1956 photo was Hugh Gaitskell, the leader of the Labour Party.

The same growth of choice applies to other areas, too. Today, we can listen to recorded music in all kinds of ways, from CDs to downloads; fifty years ago there were just records or the radio. The number of things to do at home has grown, too, with the invention of gadgets such as film and programme recorders, computers and game consoles.

Home Sweet Home

Nevertheless, for all our comfort and equipment, the best times at home are the same as they have always been: special family moments like birthdays, Christmases and anniversaries are still celebrated in the same way.

The 1950s: 'You've Never Had It So Good!'

British popular culture began to change rapidly in the 1950s. Two forces were at work. One was wealth: year by year the British people were becoming better off. That is why Prime Minister Harold Macmillan said in 1959, 'You've never had it so good!' The second force for change was technology. From **juke boxes** to mini-cars, the country was bursting with new inventions and ideas.

Consumer Society

As wages rose in the 1950s, people had more money to spend on things that were not essential. This was the beginning of what we call the '**consumer culture**'. Better homes meant children could have their own bedroom rather than share with their brothers and sisters.

More families could afford to travel, not just by rail but by car and motorbike, and even by the cheap flights that were appearing. By 1960, family holidays abroad were no longer for just the wealthy.

The culture of the 1940s was all about **rationing**, making do and hand-me-down clothes. This faded away in the 1950s, as wealthier shoppers bought fashionable clothes. Money also bought them time in which to have fun. Fridges made meal preparation easier while washing machines freed housewives from the weekly 'wash day'.

CHANGING TIMES

The first Mini car, sold in 1959, cost less than £500. In 2001, the price of the latest Mini was 20 times that at £10,300.

What is the world coming to? • Many older people were shocked at the daring new 'jive' style of dancing.

◀ **The Teddy boy** • *The clothes worn by the 'Teddy boys' in this picture were based on designs from the time of King Edward VII, who died in 1910!*

Voices from history

'*I remember my parents being horrified by* **teddy boys** *with their drainpipe trousers, beetle-crusher shoes, fluorescent pink socks and* **DA haircuts** *(ooh, they might have flick knives), and the girls with beehive hairdos or pony tails, frilly white blouses, huge circular skirts with paper nylon petticoats and hoops to hold them out, and kitten-heeled shoes.*'

Sheila Ferguson from Maidstone in Kent remembers 1950s fashions, on the BBC News website.

Teenagers

During the war years, teamwork and victory had been number one priorities for Britain. Now this was changing. Money gave people more freedom to decide how they wanted to live their lives. They were better educated, too, so they had higher ambitions. As a result, there was a growing sense of being an 'individual'.

The media talked about 'Angry Young Men' – youths who rejected the ideas of their parents. More women, earning enough to look after themselves, wanted greater equality. Rebellion was in the air. Families and the media also spoke of teenagers – previously known as 'youths' – with their 'Teddy boy' and 'Teddy girl' fashions and rebellious attitudes, they worried many of the older generation who 'didn't know what the world was coming to!'

Going Out

In 2006, the average household had about twice as much money to spend as in 1957. This was because wages had risen and it had become usual for both parents to work. Much of the extra wealth went on entertainment, travel and leisure activities outside the home. These included going to clubs, discos, restaurants and, especially, taking holidays abroad. This marked a major change in popular culture.

The 1950s

In the 1940s and early 1950s, for most children 'going out' meant going to play in the street or local park. Women did not often go out on their own, particularly in the evening, and most sporting events were for men only. But the cinema was popular with everyone and a million more people went to church than they do today. A typical holiday was a week or two at an English seaside resort such as Blackpool or Skegness.

Voices from history

'Holidays to Benidorm and the Costas [Spain] became ever more popular … The 70s saw the introduction of the student-targeted InterRail card which enabled young people to travel extensively across the European continent economically and see places their parents could only have dreamt about.'

The memories of Paul Cobb from Rowley Regis in the West Midlands, on the BBC News website.

We do like to be beside the seaside! • *Fun on Blackpool beach in 1950, when most Britons took their holidays in the UK.*

TIMELINE

1955	Disneyland opens in California, America
1960	Britain's first automatic 10-pin bowling rink opens
1973	The InterRail card offering cheap European travel for young people is introduced
1985	Ryanair is established, offering cheap flights to destinations abroad
1997	The film *Titanic* is released
2007	The smoking ban is enforced in enclosed public places

Are you being served? • *The staff of Miss Selfridges, 1970, when shopping was becoming a leisure activity for more and more people.*

The 1970s

By the 1970s, a new leisure activity had emerged – shopping! Previously most shopping had been a chore, something done to bring home the necessities such as food. Now people were better off, it became a fun activity, similar to going to a restaurant or a bowling alley. Eating out had changed, too, with the arrival of Indian, Caribbean and Chinese restaurants opening up across Britain. Discos opened too, and many more families could now afford a foreign summer holiday in the sun.

2000s

By the twenty-first century, popular culture had moved on again. To make spending money more enjoyable and easier, there were smoke-free shopping malls, wine bars and themed pubs (with, for example, an artificial 'Irish' atmosphere).

The young went to massive open-air concerts and held expensive 'stag' and 'hen' parties. Overseas travel was cheaper – though not necessarily easier – than ever before. Religion had become more important again, with worshippers attending temples and mosques as well as churches.

INVESTIGATE — **How households spent their money (percentages of total spending) in 1957 compared to 2006**

Item	1957	2006
Food	33%	15%
Housing	9%	19%
Tobacco	6%	1%
Travel	8%	16%
Holidays	2.5%	7.1%

Source: Office of National Statistics

> **Why do you think the percentage of our income we spend on food and tabacco has gone down?**

The Swinging 60s

The 1960s were an extraordinary decade that changed the British way of life for ever. Much of popular culture today is based upon the changes that occurred then. During the Second World War, Britain had been under serious threat from enemy invasion. As a result, people wanted to preserve their customs, values and traditions. However, this outlook began to crack in the 1950s and then, in the 1960s, the dam burst and new ideas and attitudes exploded onto the scene.

Youth and Rebellion

By the 1960s, the children born in the late 1940s (the 'baby boomers') were in their teens or early twenties. The money they earned gave them more freedom than their parents had ever had. Improvements in education meant they had bigger ideas and dreams than those of their parents, too. Wanting a better, more open and liberated society, they rebelled.

Pop Culture

Suddenly, there was a new 'pop' culture. Men let their hair down and women hoiked up their skirts. Out went the old greys and sober **hues**, in came funky **psychedelic colours**.

Peace and love, man! • *Hippies in the 1960s, complete with their flowery clothes and original mini car.*
▼

CHANGING TIMES

In the 1950s, pop music was for the young. After the Beatles' first 'single' *Love Me Do*, in 1963, pop music was suddenly for everyone, young and old. Today, pop music has a huge following and British pop artists are popular all over the word. In 2007, the Spice Girls re-formed for a one-off world tour and tickets for some dates in London sold out within 30 seconds!

Protestors and hippies took to the streets calling for peace and love. Women demanded equal rights with men, and black and Asian people fought for equal rights with white people.

Sex was discussed openly and the **contraceptive pill** freed women from the fear of becoming pregnant. Radical TV programmes like *That Was The Week That Was* mocked people and institutions that had once been thought untouchable.

'Mods' on their scooters in the 1960s • Their arch enemies were gangs of 'rockers' with greased back hair and motorbikes.

INVESTIGATE Here are some laws of the 1960s that changed the way of life in Britain

1965	**Death penalty** abolished
1967	Abortion made legal
1968	Race Relations Act to end discrimination against non-white people
1969	Divorce Reform Act made divorce easier
1969	Voting age reduced from 21 to 18

Can you imagine what Britain was like before these laws were passed? Why were they thought necessary?

Technology

In 1964, Prime Minister Harold Wilson said he would lead Britain into the 'white heat of technological revolution.' This revolution went on at the same time as the cultural one. It took men to the Moon in 1969, and brought us electronic calculators, heart transplants, sound cassette tapes, lasers and the first *Dr Who* television show. The world would never be the same again.

Making Music

It is hard to imagine what the music scene was like in the 1940s. With only live sound, a few radio programmes and expensive gramophone records, there was much less of it. The range was smaller, too. Most British people knew only folk, classical, jazz and easy-listening. Rock and roll had not yet been invented.

Rocking and Rolling

The song that turned popular music on its head was *Rock Around the Clock* by Bill Haley and the Comets. Soon after, the American singer, Elvis Presley hit the headlines with tracks like *'Heartbreak Hotel'*. His music style was copied by British stars such as Cliff Richard. The era of the electric guitar, drums and keyboards had been born.

TIMELINE

1949	The seven-inch 'single' first appears
1955	The release of Bill Haley's *Rock Around the Clock* changes popular music in Britain
1963	The cassette recorder and the Beatles' song *Please Please Me* appear
1975	Bob Marley makes **reggae** music popular in Britain
1983	CDs go on sale for the first time
1990	The first concert by the Three Tenors is held in Rome
2001	The Apple iPod is launched

Voices from history

'Of course I remember the Beatles! Everyone does. You see, they were so much more than just a pop group. Their songs were brilliant but they were also our heroes. We copied the way they dressed and spoke and behaved. It was called 'Beatlemania'–crazy!'

Lucy White-Thomson speaking to the author about the popularity of the Beatles in the 1960s.

▲ **The 'Fab Four'** • The Beatles at the start of their rise to stardom. Note the neat ties and famous fringe haircuts.

The 1960s gave us the Beatles, with the rock and roll sound of later albums such as *Sergeant Pepper's Lonely Hearts Club Band*, and the African-American music of soul and motown. Things became even more varied in the 1970s when punk shared the charts with disco, country and western and the international pop sound of Abba. Charity songs such as *Do they Know It's Christmas?* began in the 1980s.

SOUNDBITES
Many of the older generation hated Elvis Presley because they thought the way he moved on stage was 'obscene'. The teenagers who were rebelling against their parents loved him though, and called him 'Elvis the Pelvis'.

Worldwide Fame

The videos and stage acts of singers like Michael Jackson or Madonna were almost as important as their music. A few became world-wide celebrities and multi-millionaires, performing before vast audiences in football stadiums. Because there were fortunes to be made, producers created bands, like the Spice Girls, that were designed to have mass appeal.

By the twenty-first century, we had music wherever we went – in the shopping mall or petrol station, in the car, on personal players, on the radio, on CD, on the TV and finally online. Our taste in music had broadened, too.

Music wherever you go… • A boy with his minidisc Walkman in 1998. Music on the move had begun with radios and portable cassette players.

Thousands attended concerts by the Three Tenors and classically-trained artists such as Katherine Jenkins had fans like pop singers. An old rocker like Paul McCartney even tried his hand at orchestral music.

The 1970s: Changing Cultures

The 1970s saw still more significant change. Most noticeable was the impact of **immigrants**, especially from India, Pakistan and the Caribbean. Their cultures had been influencing the traditional British way of life since the 1950s, but the process now speeded up. From overseas came new music, art, food and even ways of worship, with exciting and sometimes challenging results.

Voices from history

'Carnival is a spontaneous thing, but it has become much more theatrical because of the number of groups going into choreography… Until such time as I am no longer able to go, as long as I have health and strength, I will go. My favourite thing about Carnival is to realise how nice it is to bring people of all nationalities together.'

Lawrence Noel, who first worked on the Notting Hill Carnival in 1973, has fond memories of the event, from the BBC website.

Curry and Carnival

Immigration's most obvious impact on British culture was in food. In the 1950s, a curry restaurant was rare. Twenty years later there was one on every high street, everyone knew what a popadum was, and 'going out for a curry' had become part of the British way of life. By the 1990s, chicken tikka was our favourite dish. There were other cultural changes, too. Caribbean influence expressed itself in reggae music and events like the Notting Hill Carnival, which was first held in 1966.

The Caribbean comes to London • *West Indian immigrants launched the Notting Hill Carnival to keep alive the culture they had left behind.*

Fast food for a fast lifestyle • *The McDonald's restaurants that sprang up across Britain were similar to those the world over.*

Skateboards and *Star Wars*

Everyday aspects of our culture, such as skateboards and colour TV, first appeared in the 1970s. It was also the decade when personal computers went on sale, starting a revolution in the way we communicated.

Many of the films and TV programmes of the period are still watched today, and have become part of our cultural **heritage**. *Monty Python's Flying Circus* and *Fawlty Towers* are confirmed classics of British humour. Interest in space, fired by the 1969 Moon landing, produced the first *Star Wars* movie and Steven Spielberg's film *Close Encounters of the Third Kind*.

If we add the songs of Abba and Andrew Lloyd Webber's *Joseph and His Amazing Technicolor Dreamcoat*, *Jesus Christ Superstar* and *Evita*, then the 1970s turns out to have been quite a decade!

INVESTIGATE	The number of British people of non-British origin in 1991
Caribbean origin	890,727
Indian origin	840,255
Pakistani origin	476,555
Bangladeshi origin	162,835
Chinese origin	156,938

Source: Office of National Statistics

▶ **Why did most immigrants come to Britain from the Caribbean, India and Pakistan?**

Fashion

For many of us, the most obvious side of popular culture is fashion. A quick glance at old family photos will show how things have altered over the years. Pictures of your parents when they were young look odd, don't they? But today's styles will look just as strange in twenty years' time! Fashion, like the weather, is always changing, and since 1948 it has changed faster than ever.

SOUNDBITES
Before the mid 1960s, tights were only made for actors and dancers. Then came the miniskirt – and suddenly women everywhere were swapping their stockings and suspender belts for modest and comfortable tights.

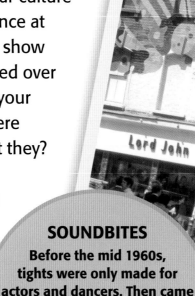

▲
The grooviest place in town • *For a few years during the 1960s, London's Carnaby Street was one of the most fashionable places in the world for the young.*

TIMELINE

1949	Clothes rationing comes to an end
1957	Givenchy introduces the waistless **'sack' dress**
1965	Carnaby Street is the most fashionable street in London
1971	The American airline TWA dresses its hostesses in long white boots and hot pants
1984	Fashion for plain white T-shirts carrying slogans in black type become popular
1997	Spice Girl Geri Halliwell wears her famous **Union Jack** minidress
2000s	Tattooing and piercing becomes very popular

From Patching Up to Hot Pants

Few people were wealthy enough to worry about looking fashionable in the 1940s. Rather than buying new clothes, it was cheaper to patch up old ones and repair old shoes. With people earning higher wages, 1950s fashion became more exciting with the 'teddy boy' look for men and either the 'sack' dress or frocks that spread like parachutes for women.

In the 1960s and 1970s, fashion branched out in dozens of directions. There were mini, midi and maxi skirts, bright fluorescent colours, tight trousers and bell-bottoms, platform shoes, hot pants, jeans and polo-neck sweaters.

Into the 80s

The 1980s gave us torn jeans and shoulder pads, while the 1990s brought in the sporty look, baggy trousers, Doc Martens and the return of short hair for men. Then came 'designer' clothes with labels such as Ralph Lauren and Hugo Boss, which were as important as the look, trousers that showed your pants and tops that displayed your stomach.

Fashion for All

These quick changes in fashion were made possible by growing wealth and new materials, brought about by developments in technology. Tights would not have been possible without nylon, for example, and cycling shorts could only be made from Lycra, which was not invented until 1959.

Interestingly, although people wanted to look fashionable, that did not always mean looking smart. Men wore jackets and ties less often and it became common for women to wear jeans for quite formal occasions.

Come along, men! • *By the 1950s, for the first time it was becoming normal for men to use deodorant. Before that they just had 'BO' (body odour)!*

ARE YOU **SURE** YOU DON'T NEED **a man's deodorant..**

NEW Handi-Grip Spray Bottle

MENNEN **Spray Deodorant FOR MEN** JUST SQUEEZE—IT SPRAYS

SURE, you're shower-clean each morning. But these hot days, you need something *extra* to guard against the risk of offensive perspiration odor. Men in the know use Mennen, the only leading Spray Deodorant with all the qualities men want. It's longer-lasting, thanks to special ingredient Permatec. A cinch to use—"Just squeeze—it sprays." Economical, too, a bottle lasts and lasts!

Deodorant Scoreboard...*Compare the Leading Sprays!*

BRAND	Checks Perspiration	Special Deodorizing Agent *	Special Drying Agent	Type of Scent
MENNEN	YES	YES	YES	Crisp Masculine
SPRAY B	YES	NO	NO	Sweet Perfume
SPRAY C	YES	NO	NO	Sweet Perfume

* Permatec

P.S. to the ladies : Buy him his first bottle!

MENNEN Spray Deodorant **FOR MEN**

48

The 1980s: Towards Globalisation

British popular culture changed direction in the 1980s. After the ideas of peace and love of the 1960s and the long hair and platforms of the 1970s, it swung back to more straightforward attitudes. Prime Minister Margaret Thatcher declared there was 'no such thing as society'. The British became concerned with getting on, getting rich and getting famous – and their culture reflected this.

The Yuppie

The 1980s was the decade of the young urban professional – the **'yuppie'**. These were men and women with good jobs who wanted to earn lots of money, spend a lot and make sure everybody else knew about it. They bought their own home, had hundreds of CDs, drove a flashy car, took pictures with a camcorder and wore **leg warmers** at home and jackets with shoulder pads at work. Their jewellery, like everything else, was big.

As always, there was another side to popular culture. This was represented by people who did not like what was happening in Britain: the aggressive punks, the women and gay people fighting for equality, and the thousands of homeless people who slept in cardboard boxes in doorways and beneath bridges. The culture of poverty and despair sat side by side with that of wealth. Two new television programmes reflected this. *Eastenders* focused on the hard lives of London's working class and *Spitting Image* made cruel fun of those who had clambered to the top.

Rich and poor, 1980s style ▶
As the country became richer, many were shocked to find the homeless still sleeping on the streets.

Voices from history

'The 1980s. My teenage years…
T-shirts saying "Frankie says NO,"
leg warmers, **ra-ra skirts**, shoulder
pads, big jewellery. Music wise we
had Adam and the Ants (I was a huge
fan,) Shakin' Stevens, Duran Duran
and Spandau Ballet. I got my first
record player. I could do the Rubik's
cube in just under two minutes. I
remember Live Aid being broadcast.'

The teenage memories of Janet Adkins of Bedford,
from the BBC News website.

Global Culture

Another aspect of 1980s popular culture
was **globalisation**. This was about a largely
American 'world culture' spreading around
the planet. It showed itself in films (Ronald
Regan, the American president, was an
ex-film actor), the music of Michael Jackson,
TV shows like *Dallas* and style in the shape
of American cars and clothes.

Faxes, satellite television
and mobile phones
helped bring people
closer together. And
when communism
collapsed at the
end of the decade,
commentators
prophesied that we would
have a peaceful world
sharing a single culture.

CHANGING TIMES

The fashion icon of the 1980s
was Princess Diana. She brought
a new image to the royal
family, which had always been
seen as rather frumpy and
old-fashioned.

Disco-mania • *During the 1980s, in every
town trendy discos opened up for the young
and not so young.*

The World of Sport

Sport had been a key part of British popular culture for centuries, and it became even more important in the 60 years after the Second World War. Technology brought in new sports, like water skiing, and old sports such as football developed into billion-pound industries.

Fame and Fortune

There has never been money in sport like there is today. In the early 1960s, a professional footballer earned just over £1,000 a year, the equivalent of about £50,000 today. In 2006, the average Premier League salary was £676,000 a year. Today's top players are not just national heroes, as Stanley Matthews was in the 1940s and 1950s.

Now, footballers like David Beckham and Thierry Henry have become international celebrities, as famous as film stars.

World Culture

The reason for this new wealth in football is simple – television. In the 1940s, over 100,000 people packed into the old Wembley Stadium to watch a Cup Final but they were the only people to see the game live. By the end of the 1980s, games were shown on TV in **real time**. They were watched not just in Britain but all over the world. Satellite TV helped make British football culture part of the world's sporting culture.

CHANGING TIMES

Until recently sport was an activity that took place on a pitch or court. Now, with games consoles like the Nintendo Wii, it is just as likely to happen on a television or computer screen.

TIMELINE

1948	London hosts the Olympic Games
1956	A football game is first played under floodlights: Portsmouth v Newcastle
1960s	British drivers win 6 out of 10 Formula One motor racing championships
1977	The last British singles victor, Virginia Wade, wins at the Wimbledon tennis championships
1981	The first London Marathon is held
1983	The first live coverage of football on TV
2003	**Twenty20** cricket begins
2012	London to host the Olympic Games

▲ **England's moment of glory, 1966** • Captain Bobby Moore and his team mates after winning the World Cup.

The Entertainment Industry

Other sports changed to keep up their popularity, too. Cricket brought in one-day, then floodlit Twenty20 matches to meet spectators' wish for quicker entertainment. Rugby Union used to be a really conservative game. Then, after it turned professional in the 1990s, it introduced matches with dancing girls and fireworks to win audiences.

Sport for All

School sport has also come full circle. In the 1940s and 1950s, many pupils started the school day with PE (physical exercise). Then, over the next thirty years, a good many schools lost interest in sport. Some even sold off their playing fields. In the twenty-first century, with more students increasingly fat and unfit, school sport made a comeback. Mass events, like fun runs and the London Marathon, had also become part of Britain's changing sporting culture.

From fun in the park to millionaire superstars • By the twenty-first century, football had become part of a super-rich entertainment industry.

INVESTIGATE — Average football attendance between 1983 and 2008

Club	1983–4	1993–4	2007–8
Manchester United	42,534	44,244	75,612
Chelsea	21,119	19,416	41,660
Newcastle	29,810	33,679	50,985
Liverpool	31,974	38,493	43,554
Blackburn Rovers	7,622	17,200	23,172

Sources: www.lonympics.co.uk/footballattendances.htm and www.european-football-statistics.co.uk/englandcontent.htm and http://www.emfootball.co.uk/attend.html

What has happened to the size of the crowds going to watch the big clubs? Why do you think this is?

The 1990s: Life Online

Popular culture in the 1990s was fizzing with the 'electronic media', with television, radio, mobile phones and the internet. We invented new words like 'texting'. Governments spent a fortune on education to prepare students for the new 'high-tech' world that lay ahead. It was a strange and sometimes confusing decade.

Britain in Tears

The death of Diana, Princess of Wales in a car crash in 1997, highlighted how much popular culture had changed. The British, once famous for being reserved and unemotional, laid thousands of flowers at the gates of Buckingham Palace. A million people attended the Princess' funeral and almost everyone not present watched it on TV. **Mourners** wept openly in the streets.

This was the new Britain, the Britain that loved the *Lion King* and cried at *Titanic*. The British even spent money not simply on having a good time but on a huge statue of hope and protection – the Angel of the North.

Voices from history

'I remember quite a few things from the 1990s. Firstly, the films. The Lion King, GoldenEye, Toy Story... Secondly, the music. Oasis's Definitely Maybe *had to be my favourite album of the 90s. Pulp's* A Different Class *was also extraordinary. Thirdly, the events. I vaguely remember the death of Princess Diana. When my mum found out, she cried for most of the day... A personal highlight of the 90s was my holiday to Florida.'*

The memories of the 1990s by Mick Broomhead from Buxton in Derbyshire, on the BBC News website.

Angel of the North • *Anthony Gormley's gigantic steel statue is a symbol of hope for future generations.*

Welcome to my electronic world • A boy shows his tamagotchi pet. He still has lots of books, though.

School Changes

The 1990s saw the introduction of SATs, to make sure children were performing well at school. This highlighted a new problem. In the past more boys had done better than girls at exams and gone on to higher education; now girls were outperforming the boys, who were falling behind. This led some of them into a 'lad culture' of pretending not to care.

Changing the Planet

As we played with Tamagotchis and on our Sony Playstations, experts asked us to change our culture in another way. We had to think 'green' to save the planet. Just as in the past, popular culture was adapting to changing needs. The country found a new hero, too.

CHANGING TIMES

When the first motorways were opened in the 1950s, everyone was very proud and excited. By the 1990s, each plan for a new road drew howls of protest from environmental groups who were campaigning to save the planet.

In 1996, Daniel 'Swampy' Hooper starred in a protest movement against building a road through the countryside around Newbury. He and other protestors lived in tunnels dug under the woods, and it cost a fortune to dig them out.

Words and Images

Over the last six decades, TV and then the internet completely changed the way we receive words and images. In the 1940s, before TV really got started, there was printed material, the radio, records and film. By the twenty-first century, words and images bombarded us from all sorts of screens, speakers and print. While some older people embraced this change, many found it all too much to cope with.

Same story, new image • The ever-popular stories of Enid Blyton have been given a makeover to bring them up-to-date.

Voices from history

'The comic coming out each week was our great treat, we really looked forward to it. Down we went to the shop and there was the 'Eagle' for me and 'Topper' for Charlie, my brother. That had Beryl the Peril in it. She was our favourite. I joined the Eagle club – DO449, I can still remember my number. They had Dan Dare on the front and these classic stories on the back. I learned so much from them, a bit like TV nowadays I suppose.'

Tom Wright from Aylesbury in Buckinghamshire, remembers comics in the 1950s.

TIMELINE

1958	*Blue Peter* is broadcast on the BBC for the first time
1960	The musical *Oliver!* opens in London to huge audiences
1969	The *Sun* newspaper is launched as **a tabloid**
1990	The first internet search engine, *Archie*, is launched
1997	*Harry Potter and the Philosopher's Stone* is published
2006	The row over the image of 'Size Zero' (very thin) fashion models begins

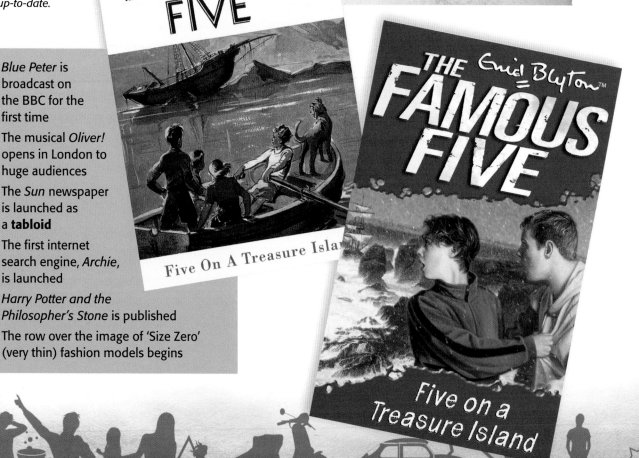

Adventure twenty-first-century-style • *The film of* Harry Potter and the Philosopher's Stone *was almost as popular as the book.*

Print

Books remained as popular as ever, although in the 2000s there were new ways of reading them – online and with 'electronic books'. Britain is a nation of newspaper readers and this habit has continued unchanged from the 1940s. But the papers themselves have become fatter and brighter, with supplements and colour printing. They began to concentrate more on 'features', too, as people got the news from elsewhere.

Children's comics, which were so popular in the 1950s, gradually lost their appeal. Lifestyle magazines appeared by the dozen. Most were 'gossip mags' for women, such as *Hello* and *Heat*, but by the 1990s there were also 'lad mags', such as *GQ* and *FHM*.

Screen and Stage

Television changed popular drama in Britain completely. Many live theatres closed as audiences chose to stay at home.

SOUNDBITES

When artist Tracy Emin exhibited her dirty and unmade bed in 1999, it caused an uproar. Whether people liked it or not, it made them think about what art was.

Soap Operas such as *Coronation Street* from 1960, or a hospital drama like *Casualty* from 1986, or a game show like *Who Wants To Be A Millionaire?* from 1998 gave entertainment at home. With so much TV drama around, not all of it was good quality. Nevertheless, some shows, such as *Morse* and adaptations of the classics sold the world over. Live drama survived, too, and musicals like *My Fair Lady* (1958) and *Blood Brothers* (1988) were popular in every decade.

Art

Since 1948, the British have come to appreciate abstract art and strange designs and images. Exciting buildings, like London's 'Gherkin', went up. Pop videos and TV advertisements became less obvious. Galleries like London's Tate Modern drew huge crowds to stare in wonder at giant spiders, dead animals in tanks and a messy bed.

The 2000s: The Way We Live Now

In some ways our culture in the 2000s was new and different – for example, we were into recycling everything we could rather than throwing it away. Yet other aspects of popular culture were the same as they had been for years. The British were still good at queuing and most still loved their warm beer in country pubs.

Electronics

The biggest development in popular culture during the early years of the twenty-first century was the speed at which Britain went online. By 2008, the majority of households were using the internet to shop, chat and undertake research. Unfortunately, this divided society between the web-users and those who could not afford or did not want internet access.

TV and Film

'Reality' was the buzz word of TV in the 2000s. This meant making programmes with ordinary people, watching them sing, dance or cook. We were also fascinated by 'real' cooking with fresh food. The celebrity chef Jamie Oliver raised the awareness of children's diets by checking out school meals to fight the rise in **obesity**.

The fight against flab · Relieved finishers at the London Marathon in 2006.

▼

CHANGING TIMES

In 1950, viewers could watch one TV channel, in 1975 three – and in 2008 those with the right equipment had a choice of over 300 channels!

TIMELINE		
	2000	Parties are held all over Britain to celebrate the new millennium
	2000	The first *Big Brother* reality TV show is aired on Channel 4
	2002	Will Young wins the TV show *Pop Idol*
	2003	Russian billionaire Roman Abramovitch buys Chelsea Football Club for £140 million
	2004	London's 'Gherkin' building is opened
	2007	61% of British homes have internet access

28

Music of the moment • *The Black Eyed Peas performing at Wembley Arena, London in 2006.*

▶

Movies like *Spirited Away* reminded us just how good hand-drawn cartoons could still be. However, *The Incredibles* and *Shrek* films demonstrated just how brilliant computer-generated images had become.

Multiculture or One?

As we have seen, since the Second World War people from all over the world chose to come and live in Britain. It became home to a mix of cultures. For many, we welcomed this **diversity** and called it 'multiculturalism'.

Then, by 2004, some people began to have second thoughts. Surely, the government asked, it was better for the country if all its citizens shared the same values and culture? A single British culture. So, as Britain moved into the new millennium, it set out to discover just what its popular culture really was.

What do you think?

Voices from history

'It all changed after the attacks on New York and London. I mean, I used to wear a headscarf and not bother and nobody gave me angry looks or anything. Now it's different, isn't it? Like the culture has changed. People aren't so tolerant of people not like them. They're frightened or something. They want everyone to be British in the same way.'

A Muslim lady remembers changing British culture after 2003.

Timeline *Highlights in the History of Britain since 1948*

1948	The board game *Scrabble* is patented
1948	London hosts the Olympic Games
1949	Clothes rationing ends
1949	The seven-inch 'single' appears
1954	The transistor (portable) radio goes on sale
1955	Bill Haley's *Rock Around the Clock* changes the face of British music
1956	A football game is first played under floodlights: Portsmouth v Newcastle
1957	Givenchy introduces the waistless 'sack' dress
1958	*Blue Peter* is broadcast for the first time
1960	Lego goes on sale
1960	The musical *Oliver!* opens in London
1960s	British drivers win 6 out of 10 Formula One motor racing championships
1963	The cassette recorder and the Beatles' *Please Please Me* appear
1965	The death penalty is abolished
1968	The Race Relations Act to end discrimination against non-white people is introduced
1969	The Divorce Reform Act makes divorce easier
1969	The *Sun* newspaper is launched as a tabloid
1975	Bob Marley makes reggae music popular in Britain
1976	*The Muppets* TV programme appears
1981	The first London marathon is held
1981	A worldwide TV audience of 750 million people tune in for the wedding of Prince Charles and Lady Diana Spencer
1983	CDs go on sale
1983	The first live coverage of football on TV
1985	Ryanair is set up
1990	The first internet search engine is launched
1997	*Harry Potter and the Philosopher's Stone* is published
1997	Spice Girl Geri Halliwell wears her famous Union Jack mini dress
1997	Tamagotchi pets go on sale
1997	The film *Titanic* is released
2000	The first *Big Brother* programme is shown on TV
2001	The Apple iPod is launched
2003	The Russian billionaire Roman Abramovitch buys Chelsea Football Club
2003	Twenty20 cricket begins
2004	London's 'Gherkin' building opens
2007	61% of British homes have internet access
2007	The smoking ban in enclosed public places is enforced

Glossary

bridge A complicated card game for four players. It uses one pack of cards with one suit as trumps

consumer culture When earning and spending money become more important than almost anything else

contraceptive pill A means of preventing pregnancy

DA hair cut A male hair style where greased, swept-back sides meet at the back

death penalty The punishment of hanging by the neck until dead

diverse Made up of many, very different parts

globalisation The process by which all countries come to share the same culture

heritage Relating to the past and to history

hue Colour

immigrant Someone moving into a country to settle

juke box A large machine for playing records in a public place

leg warmers Long and colourful woolly socks reaching from the knee to the ankle

mourner Someone grieving

obese So fat that the person's health is put in danger

patented An inventor's right to be the only person allowed to make, use or sell something they have invented

patience A card game played by one person

psychedelic colours Bright colours

ra-ra skirt A very short skirt with pleats

rationing Sharing out limited supplies of things like food and clothes so everyone gets some

real time Live (ie not recorded)

reggae Rhythmic music from the Caribbean

'sack dress' A simple, shapeless dress with straight sides

Soap Opera TV drama of many short episodes

suspender belt Belt worn beneath the skirt to hold up stockings

tabloid A smaller sized newspaper

Tamagotchi An electronic pet

teddy boy 1950s youth dressing in the style of the Edwardian 1900s

Twenty20 Cricket game of 20 overs per side

Union Jack The flag of the United Kingdom (UK)

whist A card game for two pairs of players

Yuppie Ambitious young person with a good office job

FURTHER INFORMATION

📖 Books

Britain since World War II: Media and Entertainment
Colin Hynson
(Franklin Watts, 2007)

Britain since World War II: Health and Diet
Stewart Ross
(Franklin Watts, 2007)

Britain since World War II: Home Life
Stewart Ross
(Franklin Watts, 2007)

In the War: Post-War Britain
Simon Adams (Wayland, 2008)

🖱 Websites

http://news.bbc.co.uk/1/hi/magazine/decades
The BBC website offers masses of fascinating little details about life in all of the decades since 1948

http://www.connected-earth.com/LearningCentre/HowhaslifeinBritainchanged/index.htm
This website summarises the changes in Britain since 1948

http://www.movinghere.org.uk
You can research 200 years of migration in England using this website, and learn how different cultures have changed the popular culture of Britain

Index

Words in **bold** refer
to a photograph.

BRITAIN SINCE 1948

Contents of titles in the series:

WAYLAND